ONE MAN BAND

Hi my name is Jae Bedford I am an entertainer with 15+ years (at time of writing) experience performing music and studied at the Nelson School of Music and Otago University, New Zealand. My wife Miriam & I run The Bedford School of music, based in Oamaru, New Zealand. We provide lessons, Workshops & Seminars in Guitar, Bass, Harmonica, Song writing, Drums, Vocals, Band mentoring, Technology, Industry, Marketing, One Man Band and many other new programs all the time. The **'One Man Band'** doesn't just sing and play they are in control of their own career's in this ever growing indie (Independent) music business. I would also like to point out, this book is not a form of **'edutainment',** it is however meant to be stimulating and educational in a very grass roots kind of way.

Ground I covered-

- Basic music theory.... **'Rock the foundations'.**
- A Beginners guide to guitar...
- A Beginners guide to bass...**'The bottom line'**
- A Beginners guide to Ukulele...**'Nukulele Warfare'**
- Basic Harmonica...**'Blow up the outside world'**
- Songwriting.
- Technology and recording.
- The internet as a tool.
- Self-growth.
- The independent music industry.
- Study & personal practice.
- Rock piano
- The '**anything with rusty old strings'** method.
- Bass-**The bottom line**
- Performance.
- **'One man band'**
- Royaties and performance rights.
- Song arrangement and choice.
- Songwriting exersizes.
- Marketing

Beginners guitar, Bass & Theory.

The difference between a good guitar player and a great guitar player is a good understanding of music theory. This is assuming you already have great work ethic and will practice hard & eventually work hard in performance. If you are a first time guitar player, read the entire book many times to get the theory knowledge down. I believe that people learn in different ways. I for one borrowed a guitar from a friend and a beginner's guide to guitar type book. It might as well have been written in another language. What did work for me though was the chord chart on the back page. Chord tab is a very simple language that I understood instantly. After learning all the chords the book presented I started writing songs. As good as it made me feel, I knew something was missing. I needed theory and my music did not ring clear until I had a better understanding of music. The more theory I learnt, the more I realized that I could play anything and it was hard work to get my practical and theory to match up and continue to grow. This method is to help you learn to self-develop as a musician. So, my teaching method is not a traditional classical style nor does it lack a theory basis like many other types of contemporary music tuition. If you find I talk allot about the importance of theory it's because if you only have practical knowledge you will not find you are able to use all the knowledge you possess. It's like learning a language and being able to ask were the toilet is but you are unable to explain that there is no toilet paper.

Fretboard knowledge and rule 1

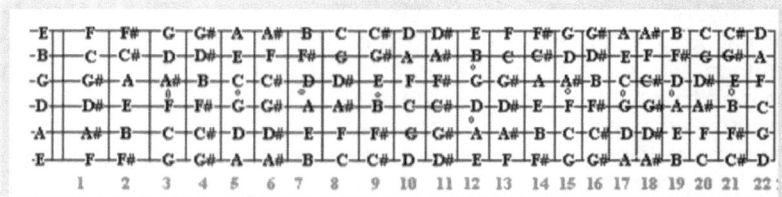

To make sense of the above diagram you need to understand a few simple rules and break it down to the essential information.
String names
E- LOW E is the thick string closest to your upper torso
A
D
G
B
E-HIGH E is the same as the top string but an octave higher.

RULE 1
NO E#/Fb & NO B#/Cb

RULE 2
F#=Gb G#=Ab A#=Bb C#=Db D#=Eb

RULE 3
4 FINGERS ACROSS 4 FRETS

Rule 1 shows us that there is no such thing ever as the E# & B# notes. So this eliminates allot of options.   If I told you there are only 12 notes in existence, does that make it sound easier? It should. This brings us to rule 3.   If you place four fingers across four frets from left to right you will find every note in existence and the easiest fingers to play them with on the top 3 strings and then it repeats on the next three and all along the fret board.   In rule 2 we see that every note that has a sharp value also has a flat note valued name ie F# & Gb are the same thing. This is not as hard as it may sound because of rule 4 and that is that the alphabet never changes.   The musical alphabet goes from A to G & returns to A.   A B C D E F G A.

RULE 4
THE ALPHABET NEVER CHANGES
This means that if ever you are working something out and you end up with two G notes one G# & the other Gb one of them is wrong. The note you would be looking for is either Ab (G#) or A# (Gb). This is because of rule 5.

RULE 5
NO SHARPS AND FLATS IN THE SAME KEY
So there for a chromatic scale will look like one of the following examples. A chromatic scale includes all the sharps or flats. A diatonic scale is a perfect musical form with only the necessary sharps or flats.
A A# B C C# D D# E F F# G G# A   or   A Bb B C Db D Eb E F Gb G Ab A
The example above uses all the above rules. If you need to, read it many times and try the examples for yourself.

RULE 6
ORDER OF THE #'s & b's
F# C# G# D# A# - The new Sharp always happens at the 7th degree of the scale
Bb Eb Ab Db Gb - The new Flat always happens at the 4th degree of the scale

RULE 7
Tone, tone semitone, tone, tone, tone.
Or tones and semitone are also known as whole tones & half tones.
Also it is very helpful to know that a semitone = a fret & a tone is 2 frets.

Pick up your guitar

Now that you have an understanding of the fret board theoretically, let's pick up your bass or guitar. Remember they are in essence the same as far as the fret board is concerned. A great bass player can play a little guitar and recognize guitar chord shapes. A great guitarist will play some bass and understand the importance and the role of the bass guitar.

If you went to classical guitar lessons you would be told how to hold the guitar. I feel the most important part of guitar posture is comfort. Hold your guitar so that you're comfortable. I would advise that in this initial stage of playing guitar to be sitting down. Standing with your guitar will come later along with your very own rock star poses.

It is important to be able to look down upon your fret board. Your strumming and picking hand (Right if right handed) should be hanging over the body of the guitar so that you can comfortably reach every string on the guitar.

Thumb position & 4 fingers across 4 frets.
This exercise will bring all above the above rules together and get you getting your fingers moving.   In many guitar lessons tutors will number your fingers like this.

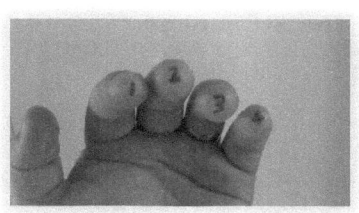
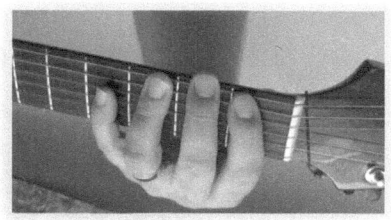

We will use this method too, in case you don't have the accompanying DVD (Available to order from
(www.thebedfordschoolofmusic.webs.com).   Your index or pointing finger is 1, the finger next to it is 2, your ring finger is 3 & your pinky or little finger is 4.

Thumb position.

Your thumb should be in the centre of the back of your fret board applying medium pressure.   This is where the strength in your playing will come from.

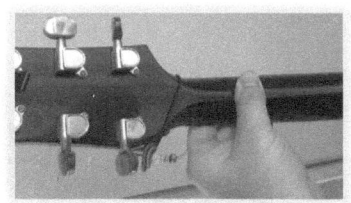

Finger 1 on the first fret, finger 2 on second fret, finger 3 on 3rd fret and finger 4 on the 4th fret of the E string.

Finger 1 on the first fret, finger 2 on second fret, finger 3 on 3rd fret and finger 4 on the 4th fret of the A string.

Finger 1 on the first fret, finger 2 on second fret, finger 3 on 3rd fret and finger 4 on the 4th fret of the D string.

Parts of the guitar

The Headstock   **The Strap pegs**

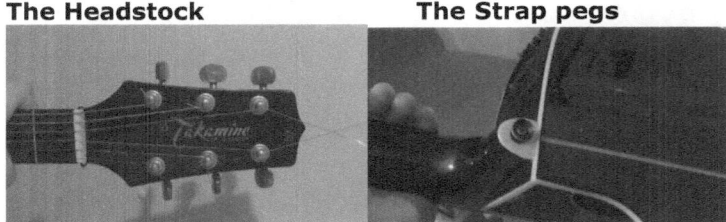

Old school graphic equalizer   **Modern EQ with Tuner & Effects**

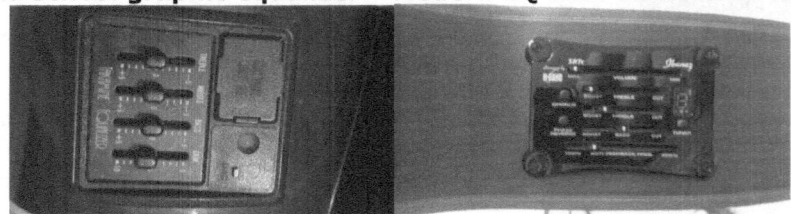

Headstock   **Fretboard**

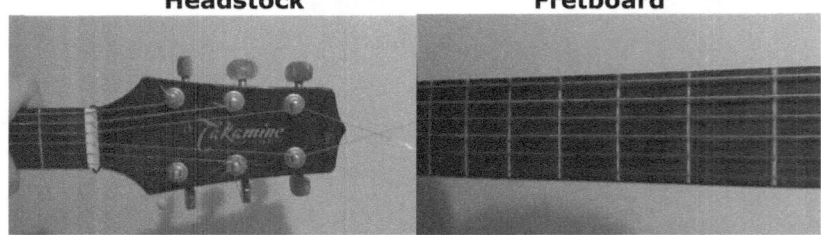

The Body The Bridge & Saddle Strap peg/Input Traditional input

Bass headstock and fretboard   Soundhole & stratch plate

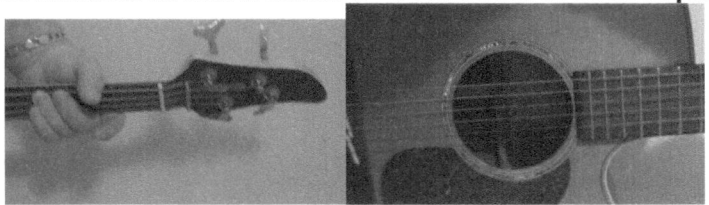

Toggle switch & Pick ups   Volume & Tone pots

THE LANGUAGE OF MUSIC

No, I do not intend you now learn to sight read notated music but some key concepts from these practices will have you understanding more than your average contemporary musician.

The first simple concept is **ROMAN NUMERALS**

Lowercase roman numerals

1 = i 2 = ii 3 = iii 4 = iv 5 = v 6 = vi 7 = vii 8 = viii

Lower case roman numerals represent notes

Uppercase roman numerals

1 = I 2 = II 3 = III 4 = IV 5 = V 6 = VI 7 = VII 8 = VIII

Uppercase roman numerals represent chords

What this is to achieve is thinking of notes and chords as degrees of a scale

EXAMPLE

G = I Am = II Bm = III C = IV D = V Em = VI F#dim = VII G = VIII

Above is the '**key chord scale**' of G major

Here are 2 more key concept I'll introduce and it is extremely helpful to understand are

'**The alphabet never changes**' A B C D E F G A

'**the order of chords never changes**'

Major, minor, minor, Major, Major, minor, diminished, Major

Scales and keys

To understand scales and keys there are some more concepts and rules to remember

There are never sharps (#'s) and flats (b's) in the same key.   This refers back to the alphabet never changes.   If you end up with a sharp and a flat you will also have 2 note with the same alphabetical name.

Every # note also has a b name

EXAMPLE A A# Ab

Except

No E#/Db or B#/Cb

Diatonic scale

Is a a scale in the musical form just explained above.

Example

Do rey me fa so la te do

C D E F G A B C

Chromatic scale

A chromatic scale includes all the accidentals (#'s & b's)

EXAMPLE

E F F# G G# A A# B C C# D D# E

CHARTING

4/4 ||: G | Am| Bm | C | D | Em | F#dim| G :||

4/4 = 4 beats to a bar that has the potential of 4 beats. (The most common time signature in modern music)

|| the double lines means the beginning or end of the piece.

: the double dots mean repeat

| means the beginning or end of the bar.

These beats are commonly known as crotchets and are simply counted out 1 2 3 4 , so the first bar would work as G 2 3 4.

CHORDS & CHORD SCIENCE

It is helpful not to just learn the open chord shapes but also learn the science behind chords in general.   A basic chord is made up of 3 notes (A tonic triad) i, iii & iv.

EXAMPLE in the key of G (G has one sharp, F#) G A B C D E F# G

G Major chord = G B D (Major chords sound happy)

A minor = A C E (Minor chords sound sad)

B minor = B D F#

C Major = C E G

D Major = D F# A

E minor = E G B (The relative minor)

F# diminished= F# A C (Diminished chords sound unresolved)

G Major chord = G B D

CHORDS

When attempting the following chords thing about the following.
Thumb position (COVERED EARLIER), Use the ball of your finger (WERE
YOU WROTE THE NUMERS) and make sure your fingers are in the centre
of the fret. Work through the chord note by note to ensure you are
playing the chord effectively. Use this method with every chord you
learn.

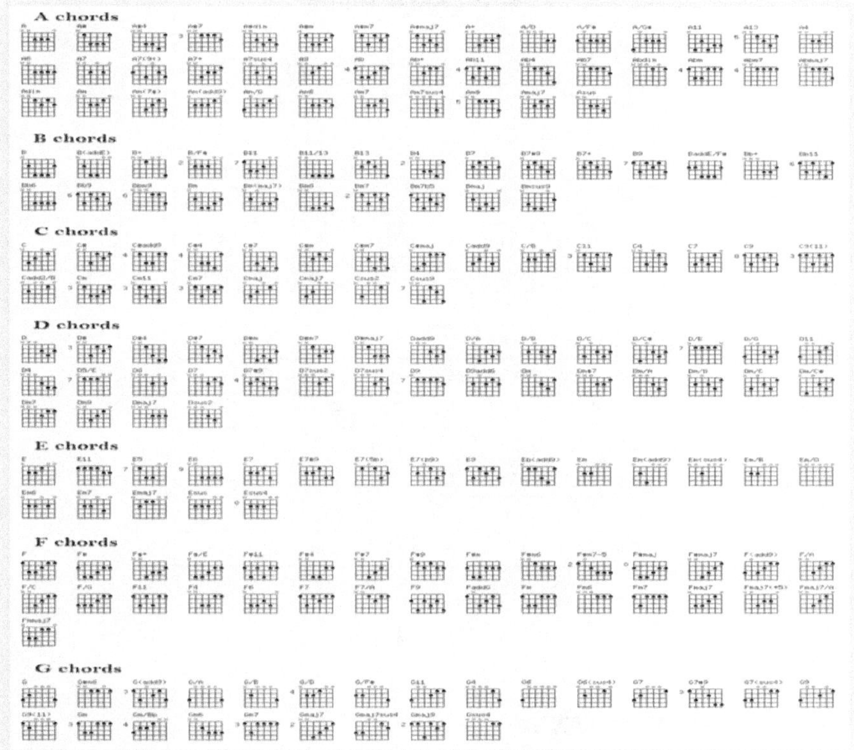

I

KEY CHORD SCALE

The key chord scale & the key chord chart below is the secret behind a
great rhythm/Lead guitarist & bass player.   A bass player does not
necessarily need to be able to play all these chords but if he understands
the concepts it makes him a step above most bass players.
I would recommend this to be the first exercise for chords. It may take
a while but it will open up your musical opportunities.

KEY CHORD SCALE EXCERSISE
4/4 ||: G | Am| Bm | C | D | Em | F#dim| G :||
If you are still mastering the art of changing chords play the first chord and use the next 3 beats to play the 2nd chord on the first beat of the next bar.   Use the time you have to stay in time.

Key Chord Chart

Major Key	I	II	III	IV	V	VI	VII
A	A	Bm	C#m	D	E	F#m	G#dim
B	B	C#m	D#m	E	F#	G#m	A#dim
C	C	Dm	Em	F	G	Am	Bdim
D	D	Em	F#m	G	A	Bm	C#dim
E	E	F#m	G#m	A	B	C#m	D#dim
F	F	Gm	Am	Bb	C	Dm	Edim
G	G	Am	Bm	C	D	Em	F#dim
Minor Key	I	II	III	IV	V	VI	VII
Am	Am	Bdim	C	Dm	Em	F	G
Bm	Bm	C#dim	D	Em	F#m	G	A
Cm	Cm	Ddim	Eb	Fm	Gm	Ab	Bb
Dm	Dm	Edim	F	Gm	Am	Bb	C
Em	Em	F#dim	G	Am	Bm	C	D
Fm	Fm	Gdim	Ab	Bbm	Cm	Db	Eb
Gm	Gm	Adim	Bb	Cm	Dm	Eb	F

TIMING & FOOT SCIENCE

Timing is one of the most important parts of playing music with other people.   While practising your key chord scale and chord changes counting the beats out loud is an essential exercise. If you are still struggling with this spend some time alone listening to music and counting the beat out.   One thing that can help or hinder is your foot. The foot should move with the beat not separate from it and if it does it will confuse your brain.   If you can't get that foot tapping in time put something heavy on it while you get your timing sorted.

CAPO

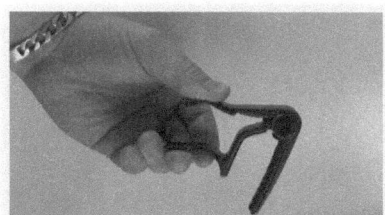

The capo is a very, very helpful tool. People use them for 3 reasons. Firstly people use them to change the key of a song to suit their voice. Secondly they use one for the sound you get using certain chord voicing with a capo that there is no bar chord alternative for.   The third reason is that they don't know how to play certain chords in the key the song is in.   This reason can be eliminated when you have learnt to play bar chords.

Capo on fret	Play in this key:						
	C	G	D	A	E	B	F♯
	Key you will be playing in:						
1	D♭	A♭	E♭	B♭	F	C	G
2	D	A	E	B	F♯	D♭	A♭
3	E♭	B♭	F	C	G	D	A
4	E	B	F♯	D♭	A♭	E♭	B♭
5	F	C	G	D	A	E	B
6	F♯	D♭	A♭	E♭	B♭	F	C
7	G	D	A	E	B	F♯	D♭
8	A♭	E♭	B♭	F	C	G	D
9	A	E	B	F♯	D♭	A♭	E♭

USE THE TECHNOLOGY AND KNOWLEDGE
I would at this stage recommend putting your knowledge and technology together and google chord charts for your favourite songs and start trying to piece them together.

THE CIRCLE OF FIFTHS

The circle of fifths tells us the relative minor to the key, how many sharps or flats in a key & what the key signature looks like. This is one of the reasons we learn the order of sharps and flats and were they appear. We now know that D has two sharps and that they are F# & C#.

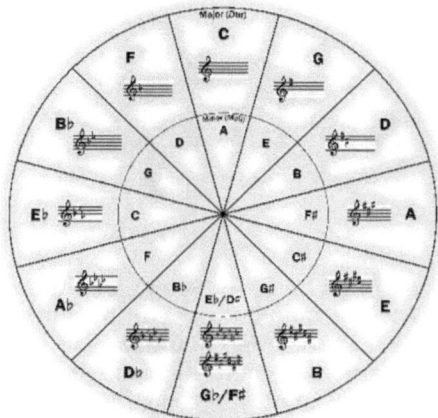

Practise methods

I don't adhere to methods that make you hate picking up the guitar but I do believe the difference between a good guitar player and a great one is hard work, research and a good theory foundation. I also believe that combining your favourite songs with some exercises that stretch you as a player will help you continue to be passionate and work hard.

A good practice schedule should look a little like this:
Scales-To warm up
Your favourite song
A song you are learning that has techniques that are new to you
Another of your favourite songs
Some research (Google some info you are not so sure of and read what people have to say on the subject)
More songs you LOVE to play

Scales
The G major scale in two octaves.

The G major scale in two octaves is a handy exercise to sing with. We learnt the fretboard so we know what this scales is and were the root notes are when we wish to resolve it. If you desire to sing and play at the same time start now as it does not come naturally to everyone.
Sing the notes with their names like G, A, B, C, D, E, F#, G. Remember this scale moves all over the fret board starting with 1 on the E string being the root note.

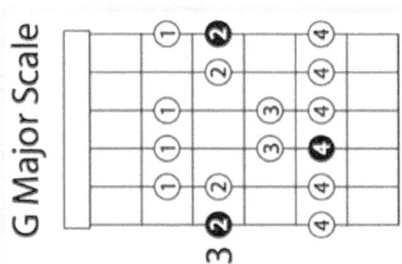

Box patterns

Box patterns are very handy tricks to memorise. They reduce a scale down to 4 or 5 notes that sound sweet that you can play over and over and create your sound. My favourite box pattern comes from the above Major scale using the 5 notes on the B & high E strings. This is a very melodic box pattern.

I do recommend trying to find your own and utizing the technology around you by googling other box patterns and scales.

Improv/Lead guitar

Take your G major scale in two octaves and your G major key chord scale and put them together. You will find a link to this and many other backing track here www.thebedfordschoolofmusic.webs.com

This is your opportunity to define your own style. If you have the DVD companion to this book you see examples of me playing this example my way. You need to try it your way.

The pentatonic scale

For most contemporary style this is arguably the most important scale for a lead guitarist. Some very popular and famous players have forged a great career out of solely using this scale. These patterns join these scales all across the fretboard. Start with example one and base it on Em pentatonic meaning the root will start on the E on the 12th fret. Alternatively all the notes on the 12th fret can be open strings and the next note on the E string (G) will be the 3rd fret. So the minor becomes the root and the pentatonic consists of 5 notes from that key. Again use these on the backing tracks provided or record your own.

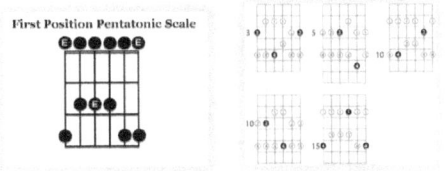

Improve extended

Record the following backing track or download one if you wish and don't have the companion DVD.
Use all the pentatonic scales across the fret board and the major scale. This is a 12 bar exercise based on the blues.

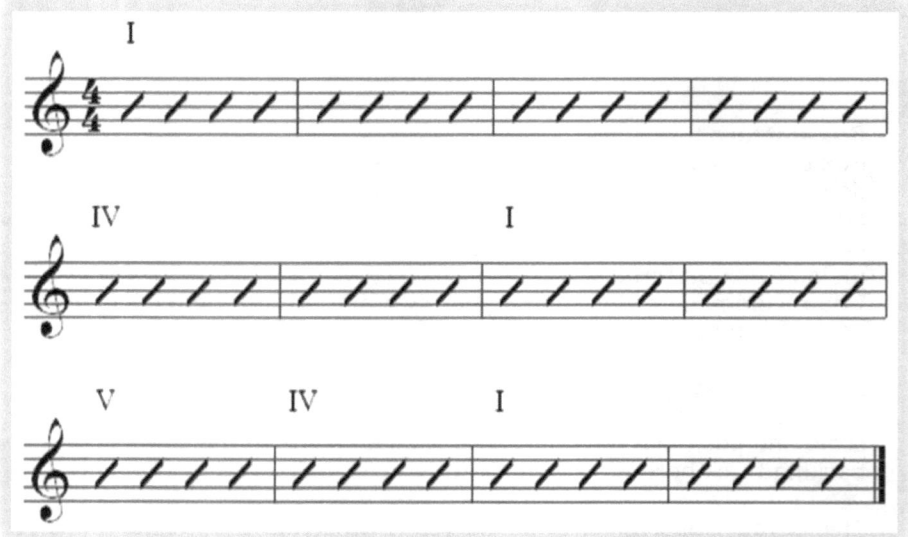

Blues lesson

Play the above 12 bar example trying 7th's & 9th's chords Try 7th's based on the B7 shape.

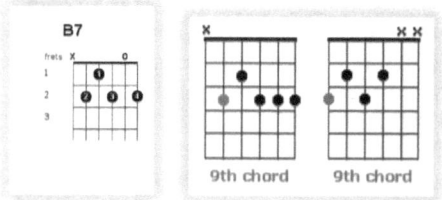

Bar chords

E chord shape & Em chord shapes

The E and Em shaped bar chords simply take these chord shapes and use the first finger to create a bar. The root note of the chord is where the bar finger is on the low E string ie an E shaped bar chord barred at the 3rd fret is G major and the Em shape makes a G minor.

A chord shapes Am chord Shapes

The A and Am shaped bar chords simply take these chord shapes and use the first finger to create a bar. The root note of the chord is where the bar finger is on the A string ie an A shaped bar chord barred at the 3rd fret is C major and the Am shape makes a C minor

These chords are simple in theory to play but you will stretch a muscle or two you did not know you had. I advise to persevere with this as you will soon discover that the pattern in one key is repeated in every other key starting with the root note.

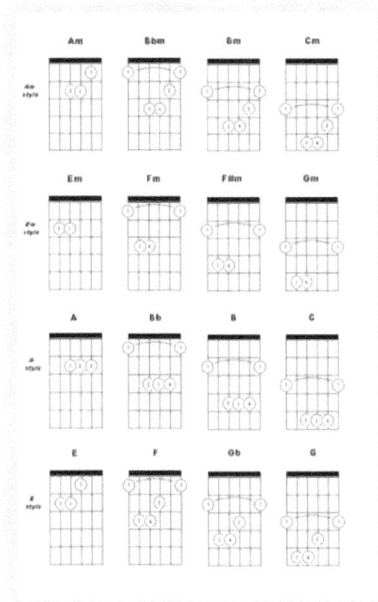

Movable chords

Try moving open chord shapes you already know. Here are some examples. D can be played any were on the fretboard.   Use the 'CHORD SCIENCE' and logic to work out what chords you're playing. Try B7, A, G, C and more

Fifths-Power chords & Melodic fifths
Power chords
Fifths are also called no 3rd's and this explains the chord science they are based on. Simply 1 & 5 notes are used in these chords. The power chord version of this shape can move all over the fretboard as can the melodic versions. The power chords are used in rock and metal. These are also known as dumbed down chords as they don't have the 3rd and this is the note that defines if a chord is minor, Major or diminished. This makes rock a fun and sometimes easy genre rhythm guitar wise.

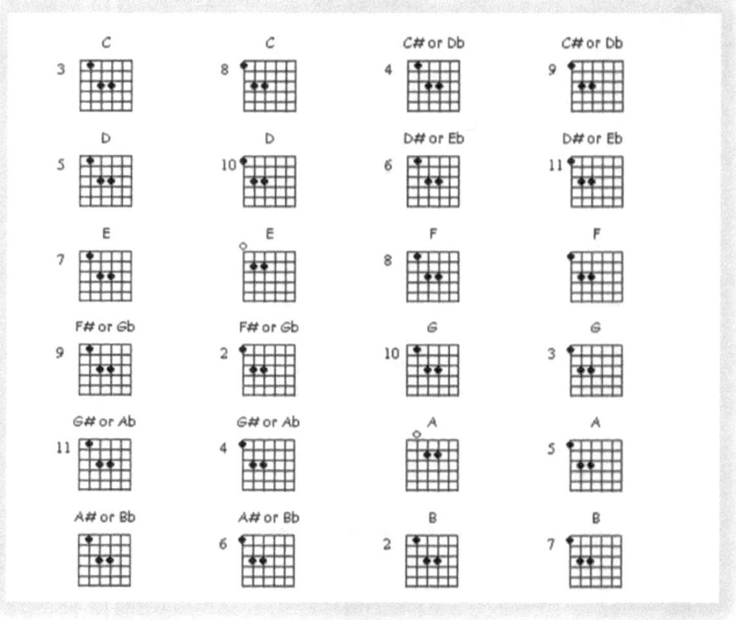

Melodic Fifths
As you can see by the above diagram that the power chord is based on E & A shaped chords and the #1 finger is the source of the root. If you think of the A open chord and remove the C# note (#4 finger on 2nd fret of the B string). This is also an awesome movable chord. Try it for yourself using Chord science, your knowledge of keys and logic.

Advanced bar chords

Bar chords come in many forms after the basic Em E & A Am shape chords. A few examples are Think of E7 Em7 A7 Am7 as bar shapes. These are just moving one finger from the original chord shapes. Take this moving one finger idea and add one finger in random places to see what happens. Then use the 'CHORD SCIENCE' and logic to work out what these chords are and do they move.   Try using D7 & D as bar shapes.   Play E shaped bar chords open ie using #1 finger to play the root note and the rest all open strings. Some work some don't, find out for yourself.

Bass-The bottom line

There are tips for guitar and bass in the above section but the thing that drives the bass is the kick of the drum.   The bass player is the connecting force between the melody instruments (Guitars, Piano's and voices)   you are the conductor.   Learn to recognize the guitar chord shapes by sight.   Learn to follow and lead at the same time.   The best advice I can give any bass player is learn some guitar and play some drums.   Listen.   Understand guitar and use the concepts.   The most important ones are
Power chords, Chord science, recognising chords, Understanding keys, don't get thrown by the capo, know your fretboard, music theory is for you too. Power chords are extremely handy on the bass.

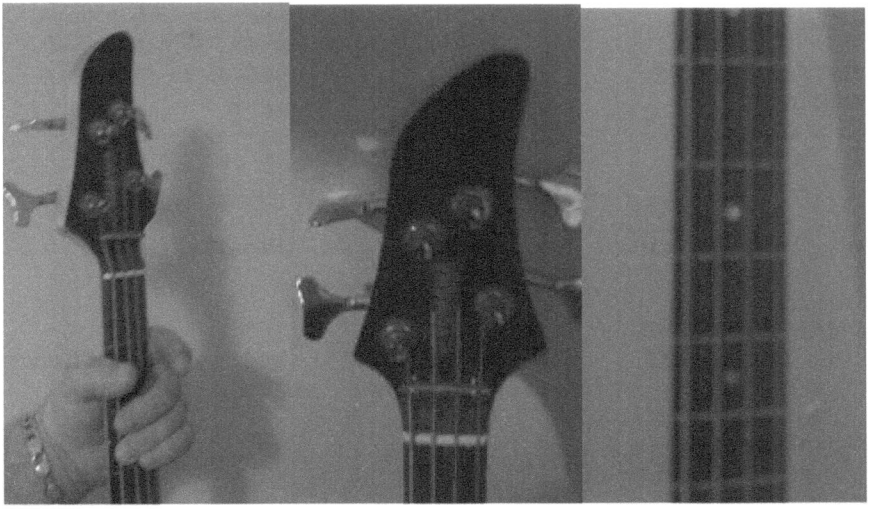

Rules & memory tricks. *(Or Glossary)*
♪ **Jae Bedford** ♫**'One Man Band'**©
'Rock The Foundations'©
1.
NO SHARPS (#) or FLATS (*b*) IN THE SAME KEY

2.
B=no #
E=no #
C=no *b*
F=no *b*

3.
Maj Min Min Maj Maj Min Dim Maj

4.
The order of SHARPS by memeory
F# C# G# D# A#
Fruit **C**akes **G**et **D**elightful **A**fter
If you end up with a B# or E# you should be in a flatened key.

5.
The order of FLATS by memory
B*b* E*b* A*b* D*b* G*b*
If you end up with a Cb or Fb you should be in a sharpened key.

6.
SYMBOLS/CODES
SYMBOLS
8ve = Octave

△	-	-	△	△	-	°	△
Maj	**min**	**min**	**Maj**	**Maj**	**min**	**Dim**	**Maj (8ve)**
M	**m**	**m**	**M**	**M**	**m**	**d**	**M**

ROMAN NUMERALS

I	II	III	IV	V	VI	VII	VIII	= Chords
i	ii	iii	iv	v	vi	vii	viii	= Notes

||: = Repeat

| = Bar line

|| = End of movement

4/4 = standard timimg called four, four.   This is called a time signiture witch there are many of eg: 3/4, 12/16 and more.

An introduction to Ukulele

A Ukulele has very similar parts to a guitar.

The headstock   **The tuning pegs (Machine heads)**

The nut   **The neck, Fretboard & Frets**

4 strings tuned G C E A. This is standard Ukulele tuning but like the guitar there are several ways to tune it.

Body	Sound hole		Bridge & Saddle

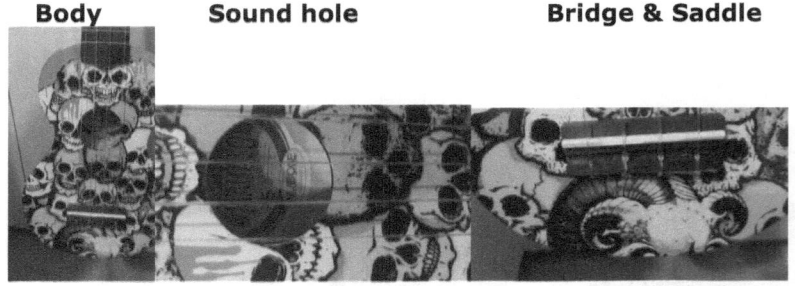

Posture-You can either sit or stand.   But you must feel comfortable when learning.   Performing is another story....

Fingers & Thumb position

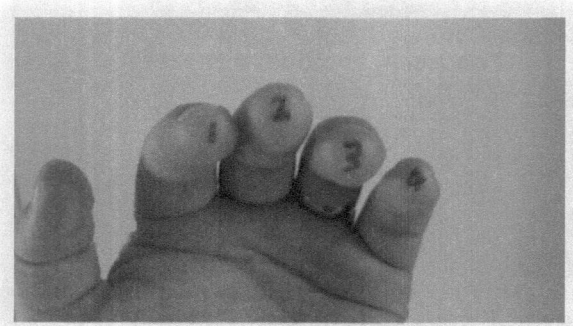

In order to learn good technique and communicate chord shapes to each other

In my opinion people's mind sets limit the Ukulele.

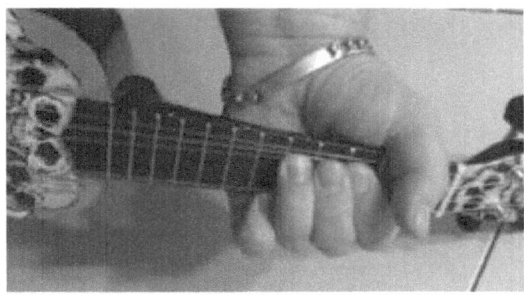

We are going to learn songs you want to learn. This is very achievable because guitar and piano chords are named the same. So you can get a guitar chart for a song and play Uke chords. What are your favourite songs?

It is stated that most people can learn simple Uke in one session. I would say that with a little bit of music theory, practice and hard work, we can play anything we want.

Most contemporary music is 4 – 5 chords and there are only 7 basic chords in a key.   So the difference between a good player a great player is 2-3 chords, hard work and a little theory.

So why not learn 7 chords and be a step above the rest.

To understand a key is very helpful. Let's look at C major it is very simple as it has no sharp or flat notes. The chord structure in C (As it is in all the Major keys) is (C Major) C, (D minor) or Dm, Em, F, G, Am, (B diminished) Bdim (& C)

We will start with the four most common Uke chords in contemporary music.

C is as simple as one finger.   Finger 3 on fret 3 of the A string & strum all strings.

Am is also played with just one finger. Finger 2 on the 2nd fret of the G string & strum all strings.

F is only two fingers.   Finger 2 on the 2nd fret of the G string (Just like Am), Finger 1 on fret 1 on the E string & strum all strings.

G is a 3 finger chord.   (It looks a D chord on the guitar)   Finger 1 on 2nd fret of the C string, finger 2 on 2nd fret of the A string, finger 3 on the 3rd fret of the E string & strum all strings.

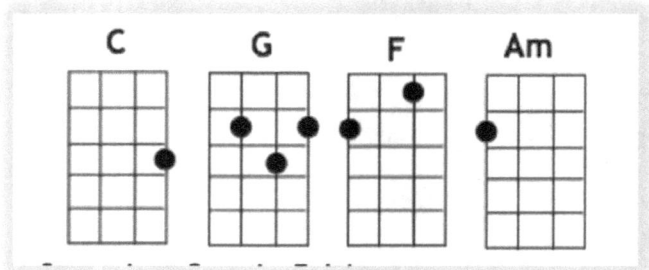

With these 4 chords and a little rhythm you can play a huge amount of songs. Here are a few examples. Go ahead and try them.
No woman, no cry-Bob Marley
Im yours-Jason Mraz
With or with out you-U2
Hey soul sister-Train

- **Lead Ukulele**

Making use of the scales below and some simple box patterns you will become a great lead ukulalist.   Here is a really simple example to teach kids.   This is the foundation of the Nukulele Warfare theory.   Some kids who struggle with the chord shapes and rhythm can thrive on lead. This also helps with splitting a large group. This box pattern is my favourite guitar lick just transferred to the Uke.

It's just 5 notes. Finger 1 on 2nd fret bottom string (A string) finger 2 on 3rd fret A string finger 4 on 5th fret of A string.   Then on the 2nd string up (E string) finger 2 on the 3rd fret and 4th finger on 5th fret.

- **Write a song on your ukulele**

Let's get some chords you like and play well.   Take a magazine and write down words and phrases you like.   You will eventually start seeing a theme.   Think about structure.   Intro, verse, pre-chorus, chorus, bridge, outro & solos.   This is a great group exercise.   Try using a whiteboard this is great for songwriting as you can rub things out and brainstorm anyway you please.

Movable chords

Again it is important to know your fret board so that you can use moveable chords affectively.

The G chord on the uke is the same chord shape as D on the Uke and is there for also movable.

The same is the case with the F chord. The F chord is the same as E7 on a guitar and E is a bar chord shape so if you bar the F shape chord on the first fret you are now playing G.

The D7 chord is also movable. If you play the D7 chord shape up two frets its E7.

Again experiment with chord shapes applying the rule in the examples above and you will find tons of usable chord shapes.

Ukulele Blues

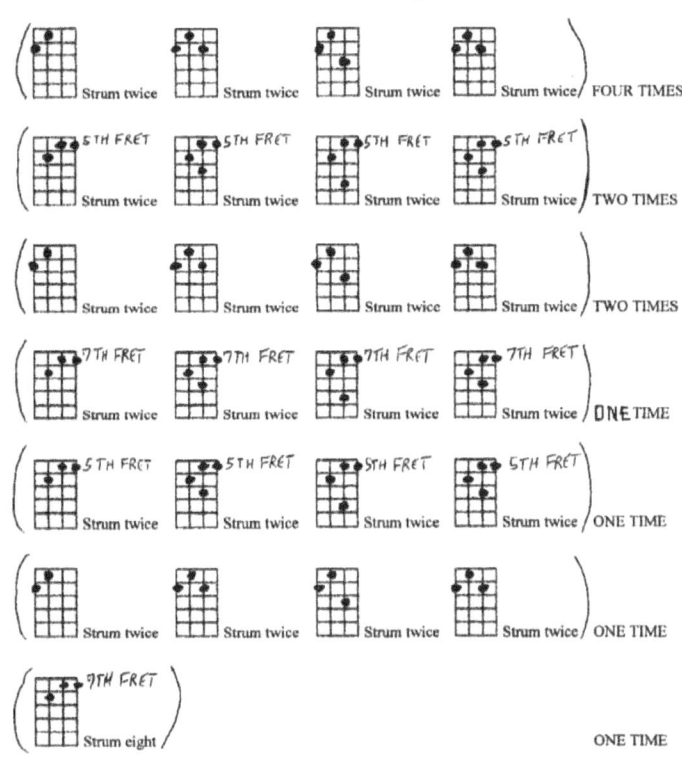

12 Bar Blues. Key of A

C MAJOR SCALES IN 4 DIFFERENT TUNINGS

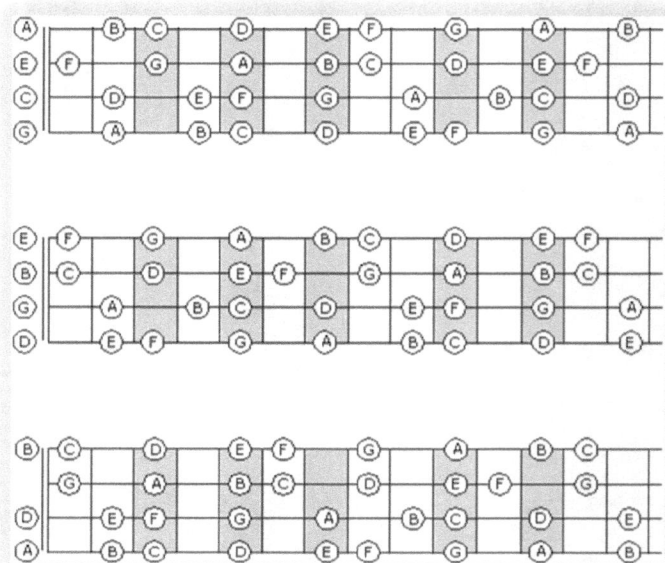

CHORD CHART

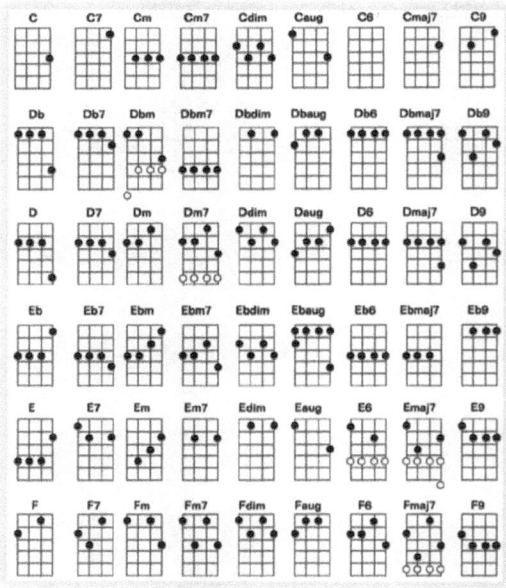

Music Industry and Marketing

You may not become a millionaire, but you will succeed at something if you try, if your heart is in it. Mistakes are not the end of the world. Mistakes are only mistakes if you don't learn from them. I met a guy in Wellington (NZ) who told an audience at an open mic event (that he runs) a story about his love of music paying for his new amp and he cried while telling the tale, because he did what he did out of passion and he cared about the effect he had on the industry. That man truly cared and helped many musicians through his endevours.

If you really want something, go out and get it. This book is not just tips bit it's intent is to encourage and inspire. Take risks and ask for help. The worst people can say in no. Don't forget youth. It's easy to get caught up in a publican's bottom line...Booze. Think alcohol free too. Bar sales is not *your* bottom line.

- **Experience**
  - Strive for perfection
  - Manage other acts
- **Take charge**
  - Band Management
  - All types of artists
- **Solo Artists**
  - Keep your identity
  - Take your name with you.

 Keep your original name or you are endlessly marketing your *NEW* product. Instead you are now the product.

Do what it takes (Sell out!!!)

- **We live in an anti-glamour era**
  - It's the cheesy sell outs making all the $$. (There is a middle ground here)
- **Covers or Originals**
  - Be prepared to make money on both sides!
- **Variety showcases**
  - Battle of the Bands
  - Song writer nights
  - Song writer comps
  - Promote Forums
  - Theme Nights
  - Acoustic Night
  - 5 Bands for $5
  - Karaoke Nights

- **Teach**

- Teach a friend of a friend for free
(or teach for us ***www.rockitbandhire.co.nz***)
- Student concerts
- What are your skills?
- Do you understand marketing?
- Social Networks Funding
- Do a small conference (*We can help*)

- **Gear Hire**
- **Be the marketer**
- Get volunteers to do the posters & door etc

- Keep in mind, if we all had $5 for every time we said 'We could have run that' we *would* all be rich.

- Put together a 'Dream Book'. Write out your ideas in   endless boring detail.

- Spin off events.

- CDs, DVDs, Merch etc

- Title and company name to be taken seriously.

- Entrepreneurs (people that actually do something) -   Let's plant a school, let's do something.

- **Recording Services**
- Start a studio, network and even just demos.
-Work within your abilities.

- **$$$**
- I don't believe it is the bottom line, but it is important to

keep you interested and available.

- **Be Prepared**
-Have own gear and backup (something can always go wrong)
.

- **Find good, appropriate, free venues** -Don't pay if you don't have to. Get paid.

- **Think about geography**
- Otago is not just Dunedin
- Southland is not just Invercargill
- California is not just Los Angelas
- Canterbury is not just Christchurch
-Nationwide (if serious)

-Once you have a path through the South Island go nationwide.

- **Don't just travel but organise things online**
- Online Lessons or get your friends gigs and take a commission.

- **Imitation is flattery (My wife says its lazy too)**
- If it helps laugh, don't sue. It means you're on the right track.

- Perfect what you are doing and go back to your ideas book. Always stay one step ahead of the competition. They will soon be revealed as cheap and lazy copy cats. Just make sure you get better and continue to grow.

- **Failure breeds success**

Don't be all talk!!- When networking **DON'T** give away all your secrets. Tell them what you are doing and that there are growth areas and you would be keen to get together and pool resources. When you know they are sincere you can talk more.

- Pool resources with people you trust.

- **Get your band mates to invite people.** –This is Organic advertising.
- Lots of people!!!

- For every 10 people you invite 1 will come.

- For every 10 people who say they will come 1 will.

- Maybe generally means NO but let them know how
  .   how great it was afterwards ☺

- **Managers get to know what you are talking about.**
- Don't look silly because you have never heard KISS or   know what Soundcloud is.

- Know the job better than your band. If you don't then there is no reason why they cannot do your job!

Jon Bon Jovi is Bon Jovi's manager and has been since 1989... (100 million album sales)   Beat that ☺

- Always be prepared with bios, photos and recordings for the   press.

- Answer all messages within 24 hours on workdays.

- Think BIG, like you are the manager of Bon Jovi and millions are affected by your decisions!

- **Haters will be haters!**   - Smile and continue your job! This comes from jealousy and jealousy is a terrible emotion that makes you behave out of character and lose focus. Instead of letting this happen use the competitions qualities to light a fire in your belly and continue being the best you can be at your job.

- **Post Advertising is important.**
- Put posters in places that the posters remain.

- Very important for weekly/ monthly events.

- Let people know they missed something great (Facebook is great for this)!

Sync social networks.
-Why do it many times if you don't have to.
-Sync to the one you like. Let them do the work.
- Be up to date with the current social networks
-platforms do offer update syncs.
- if you update revebnation it will update facebook etc

- ### Charity shows.
- Charity shows are great for the cause and the act!
WHY? Because you get to help an organization you believe in **PLUS** you get an audience!

- The coolest RnR bands have a heart for something! Find out what that something is in your band and organise a charity show to raise money for the cause.
Put a reasonable cover charge on the event and ask for donations at the event and on posters.

- ### Self-help- Positive Affirmations
- Proverbs in a post Anti-Rockstar world.

- ### DIY   (Do it yourself)
- This includes Advertising and Marketing.

- **Email**

-There are some people who have gone off email
because of the social network APP trends. Remember the .Com boom?
Use every platform available but give an opt out option. Spam laws!

- When email began in the 90's people didn't stop answering the phone!

- Apps Text platforms are present.

- Email and facebook message festivals, TV, Radio and   any other
opportunities that may present themselves.
THINK OUTSIDE THE SQUARE! Many people I talk too say 'Oh you will
never get a gig there'! Why shouldn't I? No harm in trying! I have played
museums, theatres, universities and polytechs… everywhere but the
zoo, which I would play if I was asked ☺

- **Getting gigs**
- **Research:** use search engines to find what you are looking for, for
example 'Bands Wanted'.

- **Phone:** Call venues. Be self-promoting!!
Be sure to tell them **ALL** you offer. For example: Open mic nights and
events etc.

People of different generations like different approaches, you may email
someone 3 times and get no reply but by phone they say they have
meant to get back to you and are very keen for your services.

- **Promo Video/ Audio/ Photos of the band:** Make sure the
excitement of the audience is captured in all of the above.

- **Talk to**: film schools, local film makers, poly techs and audio courses
etc they are often in need of experience and exposure. This is usually
free!

- **Talk to:** local TV stations and Radio stations for
performances and interviews. Be prepared, know what you want to say
to the listeners and watchers…what do you want them to know?
For example Who? What? Why? When the next gig is? Your dreams and
aspirations for the band, Funny/ Sanitary stories etc

Be on the lookout for these types of opportunities and if it goes well take
note of the opportunity for future reference.

- **Join Clubs**
- Musicians clubs, country clubs, folk clubs and songwriting clubs and groups

- **Formulate a list of opportunities for exposure** -Hit up these gig organisers well in advance. Be more organised than them

- For example: Battle of the bands, Festivals and Events, TV, Radio, Charity shows, Acoustic nights, Open mic nights etc

- **Don't forget you can approach the same kind of venue in different cities.**

-Talk about your success in their type of premises and why you think it would work in their fields.

- **Create opportunities**   -Set up your own gigs and convince others to get involved.   Don't wait for it to knock on your door, beat the door down.

- **Have a can do attitude!**

- **Facebook.**

- Facebook groups are a very handy thing to create and be a part of.

- Search for Facebook pages and groups in your areas, geographically and musically.

OR

- Create a group where you can invite as many people as you like and they have to opt out.

- Get involved in the community conversations and   create some. The more people talk the more their friends will join in, be invited and invite others

- Small but informative statuses are most effective. Again these will start conversations.

REMEMBER

- Your Facebook likes are less important than the reach. With 206 likes you can still reach 1400 people a week. Also youth are more likely to talk about photos and videos on your page than they are to consciously click 'like'.

- **Get to know:**
- Event organisers
- Promoters
-Open mic hosts, Opportunities come their ways and they create opportunities,

NETWORK, NETWORK, NETWORK!!!
EXTREMELY IMPORTANT!!!

Send story ideas to: - Local Newspapers, **BUT** have a hook that gets them interested.
What makes your band MORE story worthy than the 'other' band that was in the paper last week?

- **Internet**
- E studies, video tutorials.
Use the internet for what it is! There is information there that has never been so readily available before. Be a sponge!!! The info you need to be the best is there. The rest takes passion and hard work.

- **Get the newsletters etc in your field.**

Events.

- **Organic Marketing**

- **Free platforms**

- **Social Network and reputation**

- (What's new or in)

- **Web presence**
- Reverbnation.com, Sound cloud

- 20 minutes per day on the net to increase web presence.

- Be involved in groups and pages. Know what is coming up and let people know what they have missed.

-Website

-YouTube. Monthly covers. Put them on Facebook. Post replies videos.

Marketing.

- **Live Shows.**
  -Charity shows (are big profile shows), free gig guides & Information centres. Also use community Newspapers.

- Play gigs with people who have a following.
- Invite people via fb, text and face to face.

- Associates are now new friends.

-Talk to people at shows and on the street.

- **Merch**
- T-shirts, Dvds, Cds and Posters.

- **Posters**
 - All details and your bands personality.

- Flour and water.

- The law.

- **Email/ Facebook/ linkedin**
- For every 100 emails sent you will get 3 replies.

- **Phone**
- Ask for gig opportunities.

- **Write a cover letter.**
-Be yourself but use language well.

- **Business cards**
- (Take everywhere)

- **Facebook**

- Yes Facebook is still the in thing. Use your statuses, let people know what happened. Always be positive!!! This is not a complaint forum. Don't say 'Ugly local bar refused to pay', instead say 'It's a long way to the top if you wanna Rock and Roll' AC/DC Quote OR you could write a hard knocks style song after the weekend. Get people excited- some people only really exist on facebook so interact with them.

Photos and videos

-Get people to take them and then make friends with the people who have. Invite them to shows
for free to take photos and film you.

Home Recording, Live Recording and Demos.

- **Home recording Aces**   -Make friends with them too. Film school, polytech, Audio and tech students.

- **Record everything**   –Record live shows & rehearsals etc.   It is relatively easy to take the audio off of your videos.   Keep these records as they will help you with your production process later.

- **Production-A producer is key to any recordings. Often this is the part of the process were decisions are made. My advice is to do this in advance. Write down your ideas. Format you wish to record any given song.**

- **Put together compilations of your best work-Make these available to your band mates so they can replicate them. But don't let it stifle the creative process for you or them.**

- 4 Track- The biggest mistakes made with technology, in my opinion, is writing off old formats as antiquated. When email became available in the early 90's people didn't stop using the telephone. Many great rock acts have returned to recording on analogue and the converting the files into a digital format to retain that analogue warmth.

- Tape- I still have recordings that stand the test of time, that were made on a 4-track cassette. The Beatles white album was recorded on one.

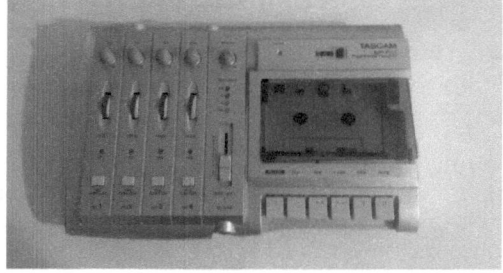

- Phone/ Ipod recordings-This is readily available technology and surprisingly versatile. Extremely handy for recording a backing track to play lead over.

- Free Apps-This is an endless way to get what you need anywhere. These can be bought and available free. Be aware that many of the free versions will come with regular annoying and data chewing ads for thing we don't need.

- Online recording-Like anything, you can do it online via free or paid subscription. You can easily find free loops, samples and sounds. The free versions of the better sites are just like most recording software without the plugins. So this is a very economical way to record.

- Get your product out there for critique or give your work to honest friends.

- Multi track recording- Adobe Audition, Pro-tools, Garage Band and Cake walk. Recording software is readily available these days. Make sure you keep all your files backed up as you never know when you might need them. Burn backing tracks as you may need to perform these songs live in an original as possible state.

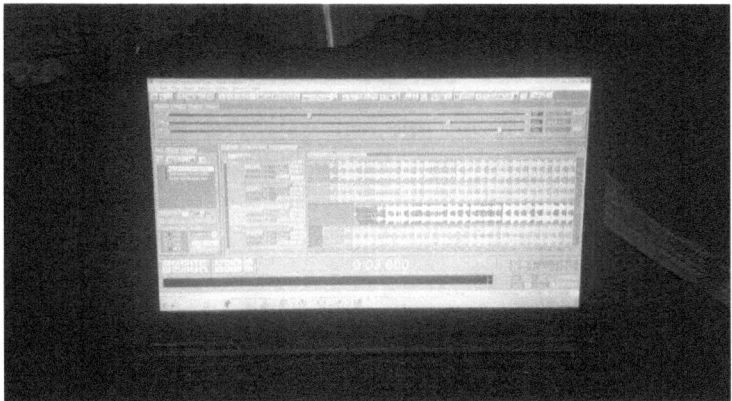

- Think outside the box-Technology is always changing. Try new things but don't be too quick to throw something away. Also don't let the ease of any process stifle your creativity.

- Video shows and Practice sessions. Take the audio off videos.

- **Drum tracks, loops and samples-** If you are someone who is well versed in the rusty old string method, then find you will loops and samples very helpful. There are royalty free versions out there. There are also some extremely hot ones that are not royalty free. They work on the proviso you buy a certain product or sometimes you still have to give the engineer and or drummer a songwriting credit. But if you get a really good drum sample for example it can be extremely worth it. I have used many amazing drum samples in my recordings and have also written over some well-structured samples. These can all be cut and pasted to your own specs.

- **Sample library-**Create your own sample library of loops, samples & sounds. Anything you've paid for keep, as you don't want to pay for it twice. Anything you use and like keep as you may not be able to find it again. Use re-writable DvDs to store and update. They also store a lot of information. Alternatively you could buy an external hard-drive. These come in massive sizes now.

- **Backing tracks-** Karaoke, midi etc-There are backing tracks all over the net. Don't be afraid to try them. Also use karaoke backing tracks to promote yourself if you are a covers artist.

- **Sell your best work**

- **Promote your skill and sell your services-If you have gone as far as packaging your product and selling it, you have skills. Start out selling demo recording services and when you get good enough and have good gear set up a fully-fledged recording studio if you have the passion. But don't stop at a studio make it a record company and package promote and sell for others for a cut.**

- **Experience is everything! Take your method into the studio with someone else!!   Don't forget to do some time in a professional recording studio and take note how they do things.**

- **Network-Head to the marketing and management section of this book and apply the knowledge to every other section including this one.**

- **Collaborate- ie if you are great at vocals trade your services with your mate who records great drums. Sell yourself as a session musician if you have the chops.**

BRAND YOUR ACT
Bands-
Bands will come and go.   Bands are fickle. Sometimes the problem is too much sex and drugs. Sometimes it's the sound, direction or personal differences and politics. So think of yourself as a brand.   Even if you join a band keep your autonomy. Be Jae & The Somethings or The Somethings featuring Jae. If your bands brand is working well the make sure it says Jae (from The Somethings) on your solo posters. This works if you are the singer/guitarist, front person but not so well if you are a drummer or guitarist.   But you can consider your band name as your band and as people come and go 'The Somethings' remain intact.

Song writing
The best music books I ever read were ……..bla bla bla for the musically hopeless & …..bla bla bla For dummies.   These books are easy reads and make the knowledge accessible. They seem to truly want to share knowledge, not just sound intelligent. I've tried a similar approach. Thanks to my Wife advice and secretarial skill it has been formatted in a manner that is designed to be easily read.   Feel free to scan pages and ponder bullet points.   You may wish to read and scan the book many times. If you are busy in the industry I would recommend it being a bedside book or travel book as you never know if the sure thing you're on now will cease to be tomorrow.   Read a page a day if that's what it takes. But do one thing every day to further your career.   Try one song writing exercise or marketing tip.

1. **Cheats chords** -These are originally designed as easy chords to play for long shows. They are also called minimization chords. They sound like regular chords but are played with moving just one or two fingers. This also frees up fingers for playing a melody and or bass lines at the same time.
   -easy guitar for songwriter...Just add a capo.

2. **Anything with rusty old strings** -This method is about having a good ear, theory knowledge and an imagination. As a songwriter/musician you should be able to play a simple tune of your own creation on pretty much any instrument. I've written songs on Guitar, Bass, Piano, Ukulele, Bouzuki, Mandolin, Banjolin, Harmonica. If you are so inclined tune the instruments your own way, like guitar tuning. (Have a look at the alternative tuning section) All these skills are transferable. With all these instruments the things to remember are research, fretboard knowledge, basic theory and listen to other artists.

   Also Practice heaps.

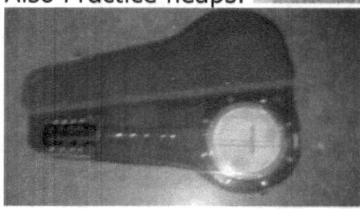

3. **Tuning** -As you will already know tuning is super important. Try an alternative tuning. Tune the guitar to a chord. Open G tuning etc Try drop D tuning (Not just for metal) (Have a look at the alternative tuning section)

4. **Capos**   -The capo is an amazing tool. It may have been designed to cheat but since its creation it has created a sound that songwriters love.   Many song writers utilize a trick using two capo's to create an alternate tuning.   There are also capos that change the tuning of strings individually.   I used one of these to create a minor chord tuning. Try using a capo with an alt tuning.

5. **Group writing**   -Recently while suffering writers block due to time and playing in a covers band I discovered the joys of writing in groups.   These groups happened to be my students.   So with youthful honesty these young people taught *me* some incredible tricks. I found the most passionate students did the task as asked and participated and yet at the same time took note for their own compositions when they disagreed with the path the song took and presented their own songs too.

6. **You can learn any were from anyone**   -I learnt from these young people just like I could learn from you and you can learn from me.   Some of the best songwriters are not the greatest musicians so don't presume you can't learn from them. If you heard Tom Waits or Bob Dylan sing covers would you have thought we'd all learn so much from these geniuses as songwriters?

7. **Magazines**   -This is a great group lesson plan to get the ball rolling. Give the group random magazines and get them to pick out words or phrases and grow them. When you have many words and phrases on the board you will see a story unfolding.

Here are more tips and ideas to motivate the writer in you.   Or if you have writers block this will stimulate the process.

8. Chords progressions-　　　　　　　-Write around the most used chord progressions ie G C D or Em C G D Pop chord progressions like Em C G D or VI IV I V have been used in the top 40 over and over again. Zombie, Glycerine, With or with out you, Superman, You're a God, Last train to Georgia, Were ever you may go, Hurt so good are just a few examples of one progression.
9. Song forms- Mess around with these forms and create your own.

If A = Verse Lyrically this is the introduction to the story. Hit them with a great first line to capture their attention but don't use your whole arsenal in the first line. Keep something up your sleeve for a great chorus or hook and don't go flat on the second line either.

& B = Chorus or the next different section. The chorus lyrically in tradition has been were you tell the core of the story so that it stands alone and makes people want to care about the rest of the story.

& C = Bridge or the next different section. Normally lyrically it is a great place to throw a curve ball or bring in new information to the story.

Pre-chorus = Build up to chorus but different to the verse and repeated before every chorus.

Intro = normally this is instrumental but don't let that hold you back

Outro/Tag = Again traditionally instrumental but bands like Guns n Roses have used a tag extremely successfully to create masterpieces like Sweet child o' mine.

Instrumental-Not always a guitar solo. An instrumental can be put anywhere in a song to change the form.

Refrain-This is a line lyrically you return to but is not a chorus. - A tag line that brings repetitiveness, without over doing the chorus idea.

ABAB-A very traditional form ie verse-chorus-verse-chorus like Knocking on heaven's door. Common in Country, folk rock & Pop

ABABCB-Most common form ie every rose has its thorn. Common in country, pop, rock & RnB.

AABA- Jazz, rock & Pop. Yesterday

AABAABCB-Common in Pop & Rock

AAA-This was very common in 60's folk. Often used with a refrain.

ABAC-Jazz

BABAB-Starting with a chorus is a clever trick to instil the hook, but ensure it works for the song or you may shoot all your ammo early.

Try songs without a chorus or refrain. The story form is one that just tells a story from start to finish without the use of the chorus.

Try to write your own song forms.   Listen to bands that have a strange formula ie The rolling stones- You cant always get what you want. This uses Intro, Verse, ch, verse, verse, chorus….
Guns n Roses-Patience. This uses verse, chorus, verse, chorus
Solo Chorus and tag/Outro section (Vocal)
Other recommended listening-Hootie & The Blowfish, Counting crows, Prince, Bryan Adams, Seal, Joni Mitchel, Annie Lennox, Eurhythmics, Dave Stewart & The B52's.
Create your own song forms & experiment with these forms in new ways. Enjoy.

Lyric tips
Rhyme Tips & Form.
Analyse songs and see how they work.

- Perfect Rhyme – Sad, Bad. Green, Lean.
- Non perfect and half Rhyme- Fate, Saint. Word, World. Trim, Thin. (Words that are similar but not the same)
- Vowel Rhymes - Boat, Bone.
- Internal Rhymes – Were a rhyme occurs inside a line or verse rather than the end of different lines.
- Consonant Rhymes- Hill, Hell.
- Half rhymes can help give a discordant - This helps give a wider variant for originality. Half Rhymes can help avoid cliché or predictability like – Love, Dove- You, and Blue.

Masculine rhyme-1 syllable
Feminine rhyme-2 syllables
Tri-syllables-3 syllables
Essential lyrical frame work

- A genuine idea. Subject matter that people do or think they can relate to.
- Memorable title. Keep it short but containing the hook idea or point.   Include a lyric statement or summary
- Strong start
- A satisfying progression
- Appropriate musical form

3 song plots

- **Attitudinal- in which an emotion or attitude is expressed**
- **Situational-When the attitudinal approach is give a framework**
- **Story song-Were the plot has a beginning, middle & end.**

Plot spine

- Viewpoint-We (1st person plural) You (3rd person) He/She/They (Experiment with changing this view point)
- Voice-Thinking/Talking
- Time frame-Past, present, future, moving
- Setting-Particular place, an undefined place, none, Scene is changing (Moving vehicle or time line)

The most used words in lyrics in songs over the past 100 years
If/ Heart/ Night
Write a song using these words
Keys/Chord progressions
How a key works-Tone Tone Semi-Tone Tone Tone Tone
KEY CHORD SCALE EXCERSISE
4/4 ||: G | Am| Bm | C | D | Em | F#dim| G :||
If you are still mastering the art of changing chords play the first chord
and use the next 3 beats to play the 2nd chord on the first beat of the
next bar.   Use the time you have to stay in time.

Revert to the Key Chord scale section for more information.
BASIC ENGLISH FOR SONGWRITERS
Synonyms-Words that have the same meaning ie Big & Large
Antonyms-Words that have opposite meanings ie Good/Bad
Homonyms-Words that sound the same but are spelt differently & have
another meaning ie won & one
Adjective-A describing word
Adverb-A qualifying word
Noun-A person, place or thing, animal or an idea
Verb-An action word
Metaphor- A figure of speech that describes something ie describing
people as being like onions (They have layers)

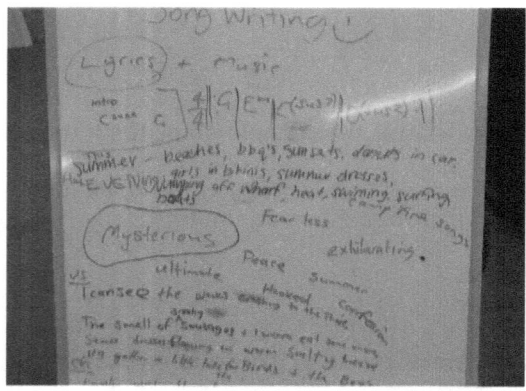

GUITAR FOR SONGWRITERS
Chord vocabulary
Try playing every version of a D root chord you can ie minor, major,
diminished, Sus, Sus 2, 7th, 9^{th,} 5th, 11th, & find other voicing's of the
same chords.   Do this with every chord & write them all down.   If you
can play D11, work out how to play an 11th in all the other voicing's &
inversions.   This will help you memorize these; therefor increase your
chord vocabulary expedientially.
Melodic rock chord shapes and progressions
||:E | A5 | E | A5 | C#5 | A5 | C#5 | B5 | A5 | E :||

If you play A Major and take the C# note (your pinkie finger on the B string), slide this chord shape up to 4th fret for B5 & 6th fret for C#5 Used in a lot of modern rock tunes.

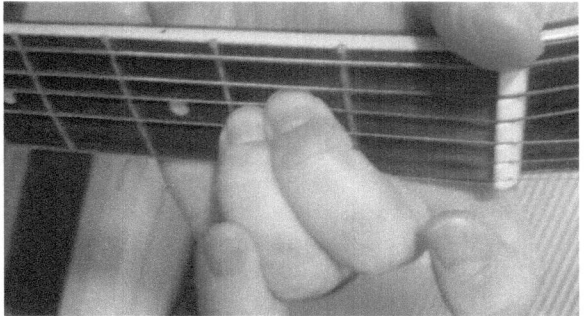

If you play E major and take B note on the A string off. This chord can move all over the fret-board in the major position in the key of E. So this can move up to where you would play an E shaped A bar chord & B bar chord. Like most movable chord shapes they be changed from major to minor by moving one finger up or down a semi-tone (A fret).

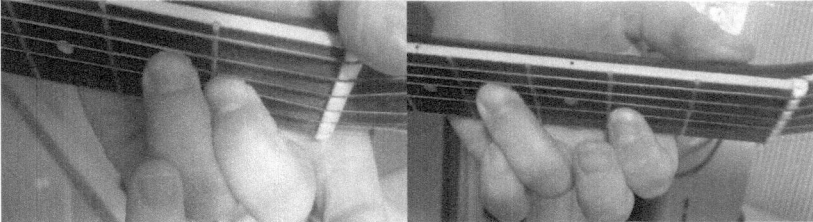

These chords were used perhaps most famously in John Cougars Jack and Diane.

Power chords

These are also 5th chords and this style of 5ths it does not matter if they are major or minor because the 3rd has been removed and this defines weather it is major or minor. This as also known as dumbing down. This can be achieved by playing the A5 from the melodic section but only play the A open string and the two fretted notes(3 strings A D G) and E5 can be achieved by playing Em but only play E open and the two fretted notes again.

Cheats chords

Cheats chords or minimized chords are great tools for songwriters. They were originally designed to make life easier in long shows and enable harmony parts.

The main technique here is finger muting. In the G chord example you are muting the A string with the fatty bit of your finger, not using the ball of your finger this time. The C chord is the same except you mute the D string & with the Fsus you mute the G string. Be sure to keep your two fingers 3 & 4 on the E & B strings throughout these chords. With the Em sus chord you fret the B note on the A string & mute the D string & with A sus you can either play both notes or just fret the E note on the D string and mute the G string.

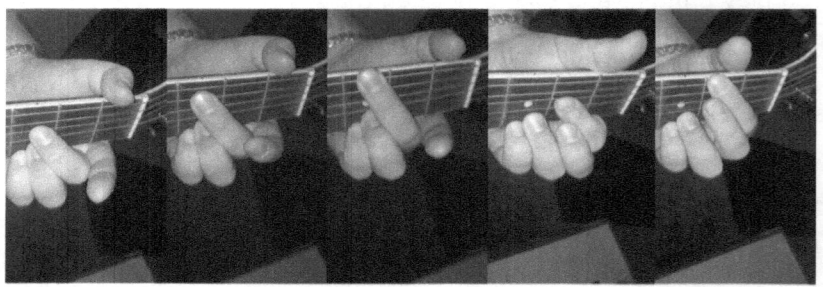

Moveable & fun chord shapes If

you have not worked it out by now D is a movable chord shape just don't pay the D string. This works with F# Diminished & D7. Asus & Asus2 are moveable, Asus7 Fsus7. Learn the blues. 11ths, 9ths & 7ths are all movable. Csus2 (cheats chords) if you remove the two high notes from the B & E strings you can move this up to D and move one finger so that finger 3 is at the 7th fret & finger 2 at the 5th fret gives you an Em half diminished chord. A bluesy E7 is movable within the key to try giving it a minor sound by moving one finger. Try some sus7th chords like Asus7 & Fsus7 Gsus7 & apply the rules that have given you so many chords. Muting & move one finger!

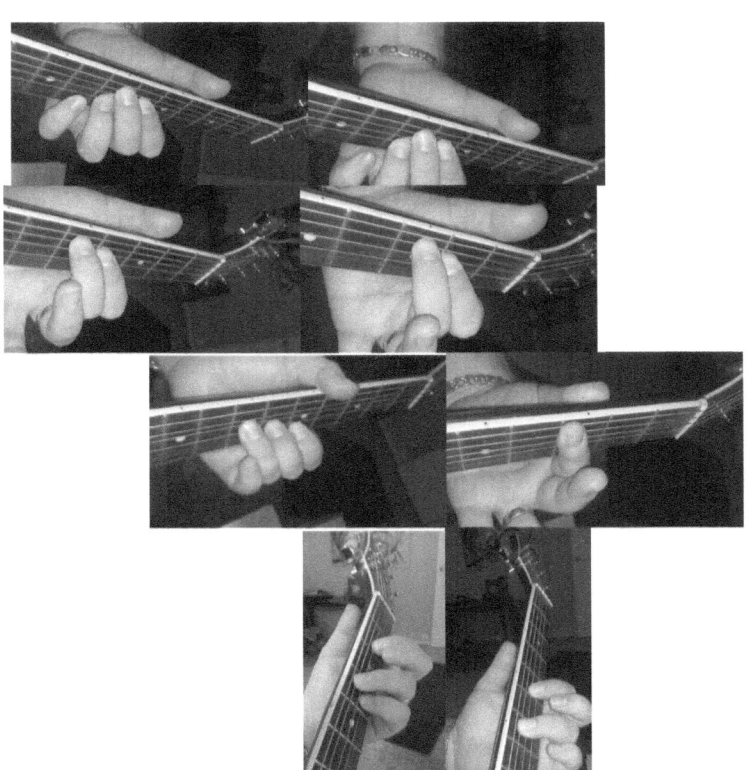

TUNINGS
TRY SOME UNIQUE TUNINGS
- Em TUNING E B E G B E
- D OPEN TUNING D A D F# A D
- DROP D D A D G B E (NOT JUST FOR METAL)
- DROP F F A D G B E
- Eb TUNING Eb Ab Db Gb Bb Eb (CLASSIC ROCK EASIER FOR VOCALISTS)

HERE IS A COMPRHENSIVE LIST OF TUNINGS TO TRY. But there are always new ones being created, so try as many as you can and create some.

Name	Notes in Tuning					
Standard	e1	a1	d2	g2	b2	e3
Drop D	d1	a1	d2	g2	b2	e3
Half Step Down	d#1	g#1	c#2	f#2	a#2	d#3
Full Step Down	d1	g1	c2	f2	a2	d3
1 and 1/2 Steps Down	c#1	f#1	b1	e2	g#2	c#3

Name	Notes in Tuning					
Double Drop D	d1	a1	d2	g2	b2	d3
Drop C	c1	g1	c2	f2	a2	d3
Drop C#	c#1	g#1	c#2	f#2	a#2	d#3
Drop B	b0	f#1	b1	e2	g#2	c#3
Drop A#	a#0	f1	a#1	d#2	g2	c3
Drop A	a0	e1	a1	d2	f#2	b2
Open D	d1	a1	d2	f#2	a2	d3
Open D Minor	d1	a1	d2	f2	a2	d3
Open G	d1	g1	d2	g2	b2	d3
Open G Minor	d1	g1	d2	g2	a#2	d3
Open C	c1	g1	c2	g2	c3	e3
Open C#	c#1	f#1	b2	e2	g#2	c#3
Open C Minor	c1	g1	c2	g2	c3	d#3
Open E7	e1	g#1	d2	e2	b2	e3
Open E Minor7	e1	b1	d2	g2	b2	e3
Open G Major7	d1	g1	d2	f#2	b2	d3
Open A Minor	e1	a1	e2	a2	c3	e3
Open A Minor7	e1	a1	e2	g2	c3	e3
Open E	e1	b1	e2	g#2	b2	e3
Open A	e1	a1	c#2	e2	a2	e3
C Tuning	c1	f1	a#1	d#2	g2	c3
C# Tuning	c#1	f#1	b1	e2	g#2	c#3
Bb Tuning	a#0	d#1	g#1	c#2	f2	a#2
A to A (Baritone)	a0	d1	g1	c2	e2	a2
D A D D D D	d1	a1	d2	d2	d3	d3
C G D G B D	c1	g1	d2	g2	b2	d3
C G D G B E	c1	g1	d2	g2	b2	e3
D A D E A D	d1	a1	d2	e2	a2	d3
D G D G A D	d1	g1	d2	g2	a2	d3
Open Dsus2	d1	a1	d2	g2	a2	d3

Name	Notes in Tuning					
Open Gsus2	d1	g1	d2	g2	c3	d3
G6	d1	g1	d2	g2	b2	e3
Modal G	d1	g1	d2	g2	c3	d3
Overtone	c2	e2	g2	a#2	c3	d3
Pentatonic	a1	c2	d2	e2	g2	a3
Minor Third	c2	d#2	f#2	a2	c3	d#3
Major Third	c2	e2	g#2	c3	e3	g#3
All Fourths	e1	a1	d2	g2	c3	f3
Augmented Fourths	c1	f#1	c2	f#2	c3	f#3
Slow Motion	d1	g1	d2	f2	c3	d3
Admiral	c1	g1	d2	g2	b2	c3
Buzzard	c1	f1	c2	g2	a#2	f3
Face	c1	g1	d2	g2	a2	d3
Four and Twenty	d1	a1	d2	d2	a2	d3
Ostrich	d1	d2	d2	d2	d3	d3
Capo 200	c1	g1	d2	d#2	d3	d#3
Balalaika	e1	a1	d2	e2	e2	a2
Charango		g1	c2	e2	a2	e3
Cittern One	c1	f1	c2	g2	c3	d3
Cittern Two	c1	g1	c2	g2	c3	g3
Dobro	g1	b1	d2	g2	b2	d3
Lefty	e3	b2	g2	d2	a1	e1
Mandoguitar	c1	g1	d2	a2	e3	b3
Rusty Cage	b0	a1	d2	g2	b2	e3
Em tuning	E	B	E	G	B	E

Tuning Tips
- ❖ Tune your guitar every time you pick it up to play, guitars can go out of tune sooner than you think.
- ❖ Tuning will improve your ear
- ❖ Avoid leaving your guitar in areas with extreme temperature changes; this will definitely mess up the tuning. Dropping or bumping the guitar will also make it go out of tune. Carry your guitar in a case as any damage to it could affect how well it tunes up.

- ❖ In a noisy environment you will definitely want to use a guitar tuner. You should purchase a quality tuner. You don't need to spend a lot. An inexpensive tuner or tuning fork is definitely good enough to start out. Always bring it to gigs and jam sessions. But, remember try to develop your ear by using the traditional guitar tuning method when you can. In the long run you will be just that much better of a musician. Only use a guitar tuner to tune the Low E string and then tune the rest by ear. This will help develop your ear as a musician.
- ❖ Learn to attach the strings to the machine heads properly.
- ❖ **ALWAYS TUNE UP!** When you tune a guitar string, always start below the desired note and tune up to pitch not down to pitch. This will help prevent the string from going flat during play. Even if the note is too high you can stretch the string to give it some slack then tighten it.
- ❖ Tuning heads have a certain amount of "play" in them so make a couple of deep bends and then fine tune the string.
- ❖ Always have your tuner in your case or download an app for your phone.

One Man Band
The one man theory is based upon how I learnt to play guitar.   Sing with your instrument from day one! Take every single trick you learn and write a song around it.   Be the in control of your creativity & your career.
Stay inspired-Go to auditions, Video & live formats.
-Enter competitions
-Go to open mic, Jam sessions & Karaoke nights.
-Put together shows with your friends.
-Don't let genre be a boundary.
-Live experience is essential.
-Learn a secondary instrument like Bass.
-Bass with teach you a lot about rhythm & groove.
Think carefully about song choices and arrangement's if performing covers. Keep your sound if you have a long term interest in songwriting.

If you have a few chords & something to say, you can write a song. So if you have lots of chords and an opinion then start the process of learning the language of songwriting. It is painting a picture so make sure the words describe the canvas. Start simple with two verses & a chorus. Attempt to write a hook. Use a refrain. The tools are all here to get you playing, writing and surviving in a cut throat industry. There are nay Sayers everywhere; they are normally threatened or jealous. Jealousy will stunt your progress. Healthy competition is vital to growth.

Songwriting exercises

Challenge yourself. Find out who the songwriting greats are renowned to be and find out what makes them good ie Springsteen, Cash, Guthrie, Gershwin, Dylan, Bacharach & Tom Waits are just the tip of the ice berg. Find recurring themes and try them. Story songs- you need characters, a plot, a beginning, middle and end. But again this is just the beginning of the process of writing great story songs so research. Never underestimate research.

To stay inspired try these exercises & use all your creative muscles ie cook, paint, gardening & other kinds of writing. These are very helpful if you have writers block. Use this as a reference book and head back here regularly and write down you own ideas in your note book. Find out what your process is and grow it. Try anything.

Take a twelve bar blues or rock n roll chord progression & write your own lyrics.

||: A| A | A | A | D | D | A | A | E | D | A| E7:||

Pay attention & listen to life

- **Clever things people say**
- **What they laugh at**
- **How they interact with each other**

- **Lines in movies**
- **Take note**
- **Simplicity-don't ever underrate simplicity**
- **Start with a title that inspires you**
- **Research your ideas**
- **Re-write/perfect**
- **Word reduction**
- **Twist lines & think outside the square-First time buyer becomes first time home-wrecker**
- **Coin a phrase**
- **Be descriptive don't just say it hurt...tell how it hurt**

Swap minors for majors.

Take your favourite chord progressions & swap the relative minors or majors. Em for G or C for Am. So a rock song with these chords A D E becomes F#m Bm C#m. This will change the sound there for often you will wish to change the feel or timing. Now the song sounds nothing like the original inspiration.

Quick fire ideas

- Take a tough jazz progression & simplify it to make it blues or smooth Jazz ie change all the 11ths etc to 7th's or 9th's that you can play well.
- Arrange a rock song as a ballad or visa versa.
- Take a well-known rock song and turn it into a country song like Johnny Cash would have.
- Take a ballad and turn it into a punk-pop anthem
- Anything can become your sound
- Find an old famous poem and put music to it.
- Take your favourite chord progressions & play them as suspended chords or 9ths 7ths or major 7ths.
- Write to a theme- A Christmas song (Christmas carol), anniversary, wedding, birthday wish, summer love or a holiday song.
- Write a desperate plea or a prayer.
- Write a dead letter to a friend, family member, loved one or an ex-partner.
- Write a sermon or philosophy on life ie it's my life by Bon Jovi
- Use these phrases- Mama always told me...Don't go to...please don't …..
- Check out some movie soundtracks-Write a song for your favourite movie.
- Write to a repetitive chord progression ie ||: I | V | VI | I :||
- Write a two chord song i.e. free falling, Achy breaky heart, Tulsa time, Jambalaya.
- Write a 4 chord masterpiece ||: I | VI | IV | V:||
- Try 5 chords ||: I | V | II | V | I :|| or chords ||: I | V | II | IV | III :||
- Try 6 chords ||: I | V | II | IV | III | VII :||

- Try creating your own chord shapes ie take your favourite chords & add or take a finger away.
- Keep the root chord and move the bass line D D/G D/F# D/B D
- Coin a phrase ie take light as a feather and say light as a flake or as heavy as a….
- Turn the TV on only long enough to catch one phrase and write around it
- Write around your favourite movie titles
- Research- Write a biography on a famous person…It's been done before…
- Write around song titles i.e. take a box set or anthology or go to iTunes and get tittles…but don't use the most famous or recognizable title…
- Modulate- from C to G ie C Em F G Am Em Bm G Or go there and modulate back C Em F G Am Em Bm G C F G…In this example C pivots on Am onto Em, the relative of G…Try this in other keys.
- Try using bar chords instead of open chords and add fingers in or take fingers off…
- Try new chord voicing's i.e. the basic tonic triad of D is d f# a so find these notes in other places were the notes are close together and then you have a new voicing.   Get to know your fretboard…
- Try these easy moveable chord shapes C D G E F A
- Try G Csus2 Dsus2 G/B Dsus
- Write around your favourite poem.
- Write a song on another instrument 'Anything with rust old strings' method
- Write a biography of who you could have been if you had or hadn't…
- Use a person's name.   Not someone you know unless it's a nice sentiment.
- Write a song about your idol/hero from a truly personal point of view
- Write a song for the coolest band in your hometown
- Write a hangover song, Cowboy song or train song
- Write a song regarding an episode of your favourite TV show
- Write a news report
- Write a song based on unfounded gossip
- Write from a book or movie tittle
- Write about a taxi driver, lawyer or Waitress
- Write about meeting your high school sweet heart or a blind date 10 years later
- Write a big/long rock opera i.e. Bohemian rhapsody, November Rain, Stairway to heaven, American pie & Jesus of suburbia
- Write a national anthem
- Write a blues song using an AAB structure
- Try these chord progressions I IV V, VI IV I V, I IV VI V

- Write a Christmas song, Birthday song, Anniversary or Wedding song
- Write a song based on a headline
- Write a bible story into a song…The best book of all time
- Try No Chorus, No rhymes
- Toxic combinations i.e. Tequila and Women
- Try over used words & themes. Lonesome, Always, Alone, Amazing, Today, Goodbye, Easy, Money & Sorry.
- Write a trilogy with combined themes
- Change all the chords to dominant 7ths Using II III V IV
- Write about a cartoon character or superhero or a pro wrestler…i.e. Honky tonk man, Mickey Mouse or Superman
- Write an Obituary or Eulogy
- Write an antidote i.e. Granddad's motto always ways…
- Use the song tittle once
- Write over a backing track
- Try a pre-Chorus
- A recollection i.e. I remember
- A 10 minute song
- Write a blues, smooth jazz, gospel, kids, or funny song
- A seasonal song i.e. summer, Autumn, winter or spring
- Write a song to be played at your funeral
- Returning to your home-town after 10 years
- Unrequited love
- Thank someone for destroying your life
- Write a song using just one chord in the Verses
- Substitute the chords ie use suspended, 9th or 7th chords
- Write a song about your ex's bad habits or sarcastically how music you miss them
- Re-write that movie ending that has always annoyed you.
- Write a sports theme
- Write a political song
- Take a song you disagree with and re-write it
- Write a song about how you've grown up
- Do you regret? If so why. If not why?
- Write an answer song i.e. put yourself in the shoes of the person being sung about
- Write a song around a riff
- Write a song for a famous band. Try to make it sound like them
- What is your motto to life ie what have you learnt the hard way
- Write a teen angst anthem
- Change the time period of the song ie then I felt, rather than it feels like & see what happens
- Write a song about road life
- Write a new lyric or melody over a karaoke track
- Write a typically over used country, blues, rock or pop chord structure
- Find sheet music or chord chart to a song you've never heard and write a melody

- Write a song from someone else's point of view...i.e. a friends tragic relationship
- Take a song from your repertoire and change the genre

Collaboration

Ask a friend to team up on collaboration. There are many ways of collaborating. One is a process of sacrificing for the benefit of the song. One is blind faith. Send someone away with your unfinished work. Write with a band. Grab a friend's poem and write a song with it.

Hints

50 years after the death of an author a song becomes public (Creative commons) this means you can utilize it in your creativity but don't let it limit your creativity.

Presidential speeches belong to we the people....I had a dream...yes its been done to death but now you know why...

The most common question asked of songwriters is 'do you write the words or music first'. To songwriters this seems like a dumb question but in reality it is quite telling in regards to your progress. No matter what your answer is, turn your process around and try to write a poem or alternatively if you write the music first.

Research Get to know your fretboard Listen to other genres Read a lot (Start with this book)   learn all the instruments in this book

ROCK PIANO FOR SONGWRITERS

This is as simple as a little theory you have learnt in the guitar/theory section. Remember all the white notes is the key of C. The black notes are the sharp/flat notes. So take the tonic triad theory and play 1 3 5 i.e. A C chord is c e g.... C Key chord chart is all the basic chords in C major.

C Dm Em F G Am Bdim C -learn to play that and move onto G(G has one sharp f#). Research, you can learn to play any instrument easily online.

Chords, melody & Bass

You can play chords with one hand and a melody or riff with the other hand.   Remember if you're in C you can play the melody or riff in an ad lib style to get used to it.   You can also play the bass notes with one hand and the chords or melody with the other.   You can also play two note chords in the bass area of the piano (Low left) using the root and the third.   Experiment and research. This simple, beginners may seem easy but there is a lot to becoming a great pianist.   But in Contemporary music less can be more.

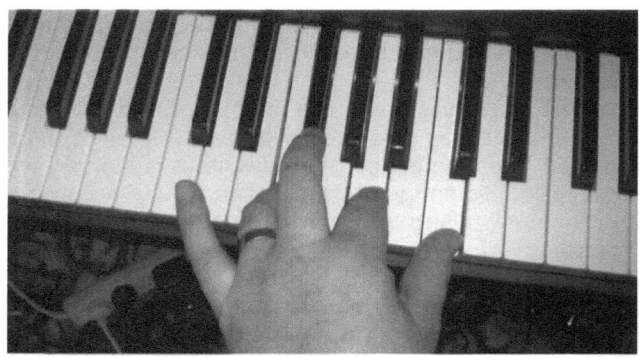

HARMONICA BASICS

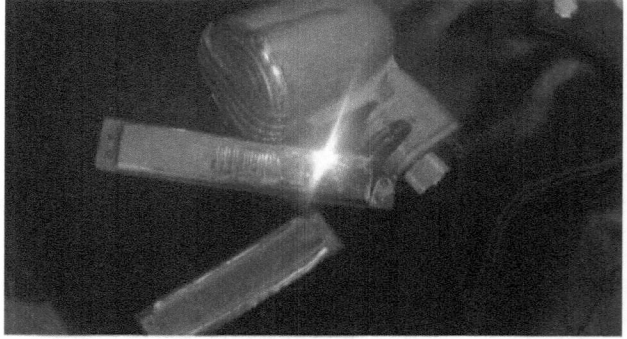

The harmonica is probably the most underrated instrument known to man today.   It has been relegated to the kiddies toy box.   Everyone has owned one or played one. One of the things that slows its progress back into popularity is the inability to share the instrument.   Yes it is a very unhygienic thing to be in a kid's toy box. I had one from a very young age but it did not make sense to me as a stand-alone instrument. From the moment I slung it around my neck and strummed the guitar with it I was in love with the harmonica. Once you have found this love you are now in the club and may refer to it as your harp.   The term mouth organ was once its official name but that's not the most Rock n Roll of names.

Yes **the Harmonica is** a **Rock** instrument.   It is also very at home in blues, country & smooth Jazz.   That being said there are no genre restrictions I'd buy into.   I've heard great harmonica solos in rap.   For differing reasons I own 18 harmonicas in different keys for qualities and sounds.   A cheaper harmonica can be bought for less than $20 NZD and they are reasonable quality.   The more you pay the better the quality.   I would advise once you are taking it seriously to buy a set of harmonicas. They often come in a stylish box and it is cheaper to buy them in that sort of quantity.   This will give you more keys to play.   If you play guitar I'd seriously advise buying a neck holder.   You at least need harmonicas in the following key to jam or play in a band- C G E A D Bb F

The Diatonic harp
The diatonic harp has every note in a key. This means it's like an automatic car it changes gears for you.   So you can safely play every note on your harp.
The Chromatic harp
The Chromatic harp includes all sharp and flat notes possible.   This needs you to be great with music theory or have a great ear. The Chromatic harp is definitely not a beginner's harp.   So we will deal mostly with diatonic harp in this book.
Straight Harp & Cross harp
There are many ways to play the Harmonica- Straight Harp, Cross Harp, Gypsy Harp and many, many more.   Maybe you'll come up with your own.
Play along with blues jams on youtube that tell you what key they are playing in if you don't have the type of ear that tells you what key a piece is in.

Tools of the trade-
    10. Harmonica(S)
    11. One man band book
    12. Imagination
    13. Backing tracks or a guitar, Piano or whatever you play.
The key of your harp-

You will find on your harmonica the key is written.   Normally this is written on the right hand side.

Straight Harp (Position 1)

So if your harp has a C written on it then you can use this harp in the key of C for straight harp. Straight harp is where you play the melody (Like a vocal part).

Cross Harp

Cross harp is where you play safe notes in a different key than your harp. There are many different positions of cross harp.

Technique & Tips
- **Breathe**

So firstly breathe naturally. This will help you play in a controlled manner and you will sound more natural.

- **Lips**

Keep your lips moist to help the harp slide back and forth between your lips.

Don't hold your lips too tight.

- **Saliva**

Try not to let your harp fill with saliva.   This is very disgusting and unhygienic.   It will also reduce the life of your hap by rusting the reeds.

- **Blow**

This self-explanatory but do so gently.

- **Draw**

This means to suck but again do so gently or you will suck while drawing.

Keep your harp in its case so that you don't get dirt or fluff from your pockets in it.   This will jam the harp.

- **Single note pucker**

This is where you will gain control of the instrument. Pucker up like a kiss. Don't use your tongue to help you find the note.

- **PRACTICE, PRACTICE, PRACTICE.**
- **Tonguing**

This is simply created by saying "ta ta ta" while drawing or blowing. Try it fast and slow.   Try mouthing other words of your own creating like fire or take words from the song. This will give you the correct rhythm. This also creates percussion in your playing.

- **Hands**

This is simply how you hold and cup the harp.   Use your hands to create a wah sound.   Experiment with this. Again draw and blow with this technique.   Make sure when you want the sound unaffected return to a tight strong hand position.   Also try fluttering your hands.   Do this on holes 4 & 5 for a train sounds.

Cross harp position 2
With your C harp play (Or backing track) in the key of G
Safe notes
The notes to play for this are 1 draw 2 draw 3 blow & draw 4 draw 6 blow and draw
Cross harp is a blues sound.   This can be used successfully in blues, rock, and country, folk and smooth jazz.
There are new techniques I would advise experimenting with here and they are called bend, choke & wail.   As you play and listen to other players these descriptions will all make sense. These techniques are all garnered using the previous tricks using your tongue and draw and blow styles.   This will open the door to sounding like a pro. This is easy and sounds awesome.
Steppingstone notes
1 blow 2 blow 4 blow 5 blow and draw

Resolution(R) and wailing (W)
(W)1 draw (R)2 draw 3 (R)blow & (W)draw 4 (W)draw 6 (R)blow & (W)draw
Resolution is a finishing or completing sound while wailing will keep the sound hanging. Or simply put Wailing =?   &   Resolution =!   So play with the emotion in this technique.
Blues riffs
(B)=Blow (D)=Draw
3 (B) 3 (D) 4 (B) 4 (D)   4 (D) 4 (B) 3 (D) 3 (B)
Use your imagination and come up with your own riffs.

More on Cross harp
6 (D) = Wail
6 (B) = Resolution
5 (D) = Steppingstone
5 (B) = Steppingstone
4 (D) = Wail
4 (B) = Steppingstone
3 (D) = Wail
3 (B) = Resolution
2 (D) = Resolution
2 (B) = Steppingstone
1 (D) = Wail
1 (B) = Steppingstone
The ambulance technique
So like a child an make a Weee Ouuuu sound like an ambulance
Change the shape of your mouth like your whistling.

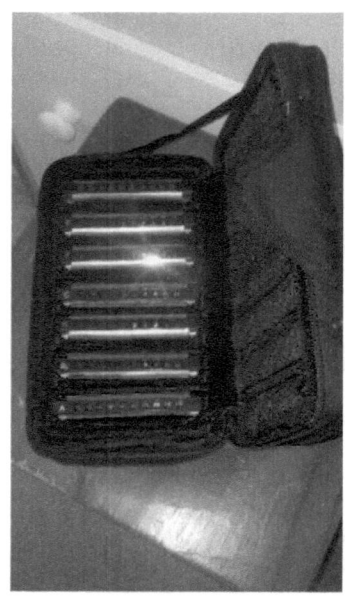

Cross harp or Second position

Backing in the key of	Harp in the key of
A	D
Bb	Eb
B	E
C	F
Db	F#
D	G
Eb	Ab
E	A
F	Bb
F#	B
G	C

So now you can see why harp players have so many harps.

Position 3

Guitar	Harp
E	D
A	G
G	F
D	C
C	Bb
F#	E

Position 4

Guitar	Harp
E	C
A	F
D	Bb
B	G
G#	E
C#	A
F#	D

GYPSY HARP

This is 2nd position but the guitar is playing in a minor key. Try it. Very Bruce Springsteen in style.

The harp below is diatonic with several octaves. These have a great full sound.

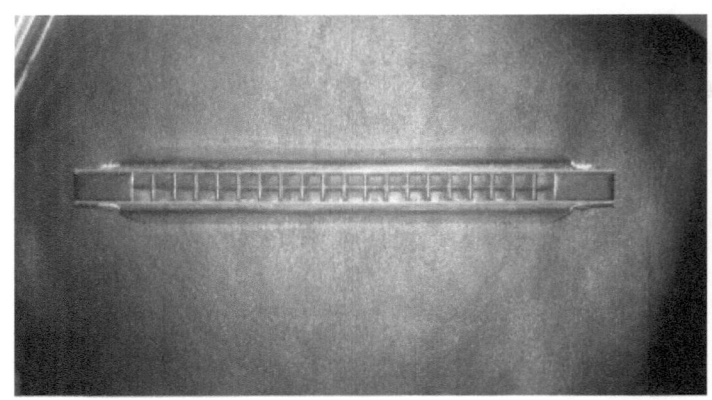

Parting advice
Harmonica
Get an amp (or a DI box), effect pedals an old school looking
microphone & Experiment.   Go to jam sessions and rock out.   Research
& listen to the greats.   Some of them use several harps in one song.

Stringed instruments
Get out and play live.   Practice heaps. Get to know your fret board.
Research & listen to the greats.

Recording
Don't get caught up in the idea that something is antiquated technology.
Use it and discover the warmth and qualities or analogue. But don't
forget how versatile and how easy digital is to share and collaborate.

Industry & Marketing
Don't limit yourself ever.   If you fall down get back up and reinvent the
wheel.   Keep in touch with that note book.

Experience & performance
Advice I give my performance and School of rock students is go to jam
nights, Open mics even Karaoke events. Take those opportunities that
come up to perform at events etc.   Take the experience while it's on
offer.   Research the great performers and imitate them in order to learn
tricks and how YOU perform.   I am an avid pro wrestling fan. These
great entertainers have it all performance at the highest levels. They
are actors, athletes & have the charisma of rock stars.   You can learn
performance trick off all types of entertainment. Even cartoons know
how to pull the heart strings.   The most successful & engaging pro
wrestling characters are their own personalities with the volume turned
up to full. Use this method to create your on stage character but don't
let this dominate your real life character.

Personal practice
**Getting this right can be an art form.   Don't beat yourself up but
don't slack off either. The most successful practice is one you
work your-self out but also have fun. So have a piece you warm
up on that makes you feel good about your playing too.   Then hit
some scales and hit them hard. Move onto a piece that stretches
you a bit.   Work hard at this piece by piece and before it gets
you down if you're not making progress, get back to the piece
that builds you up.   Attempt to do this daily.**

Theory

Like anything theory takes a lot of perseverance. I am an avid promoter of theory but it was not always a love of mine and I am still learning, in fact I think I will always be learning. I sat up to level 7 royal school of music grades and two certificate courses before heading to university and choosing to sit through music 191 (cabbage music). This took me right back to the basics for example what a crotchet is. This created a truly solid foundation for my musical future. I believe taking this course was really important to filling in the gaps in my knowledge and I advise you to read, listen to and watch the theory parts of this book/DVD thoroughly many many times.

Theory truly makes it all work. If you have ever watched someone play and you have thought I am technically as good, if not better than them but it seems like they know something I don't. Well the chances are they do. They probably know a lot of theory. NEVER Underestimate theory! Theory, fret board knowledge, hardworking practice techniques, great technical skills and theory are the basis of an amazing musical future.

You're Sound

Well it's not for me to say what your sound should be but I do know that you will find it with age and experience. Go out and play in bands outside of the area of what you think your genre maybe. There is no substitute for hard work and experience. Most of all have fun. If it's not fun then find an act that is. If you are a multi-instrumentalist, then play in many bands on many different instruments. Sometimes your sound is what you are running from.

THE BEDFORD'S

Acknowledgements and Thank-you's
The Big Man, Miriam my amazing wife, Bella my beautiful
daughter for ripping up and possibly eating my notes. Without
you bubba this book would be quite different ☺ Mum and Dad, My
amazing mum and dad in law Vi and Steve Craig, Kit and Kaye
Grenon, Gary... (Head man at Vision College, Chch). Youth Town
(Mike, Anika and Alice), Deirdre and Mark at Mainstreet Music,
Oamaru. The Nelson School of Music. The Otago University Music
Department, Akona Te Rangatahi. Jack Kiku, Louis Bragg, Patrick
Little. All my students for all the times I have tested these
themes on you. Jill and Rusty, Baz, Mark Reeve, Malcolm Dixon
Apra, The Gold guitar awards, Ian Chapman, Don McGlassion,
Shona Laing, Every Musician I ever learnt from and worked with,
Simon Tester, Jesse 'Vince' Hewit, Thomas Coffey, Jesse O'Brien,
Gary Moss, Dan Orr, , Willie McArthur, Stark Craving- Mark and
Pete Rowley, Joe Strandeven, The Heights, GD. Mantis, The Jam
Jar and Team, Rockitband hire, Rockit Events, Song Poets Corner
Music and The Bedford School of Music.

Photos
Miriam Bedford.   Jae Bedford.   Alice Hore.   Sarah Everard.   Anika
McClennan.   Waitaki Herald.   Phillip Merry.   Vi Craig.   Plus video
stills.

ISBN-13: 978-1491032053

www.ingramcontent.com/pod-product-compliance
Lightning Source LLC
Chambersburg PA
CBHW02125228052б
45784CB00005B/2340